THE WEAPONS ENCYCLOPÆDIA
TANK AIRCRAFT AFV SHIP ARTILLERY VEHICLES SECRET WEAPON

TWE-032 ENG

GERMAN EXPERIMENTAL TANKS VOL. I

THE WEAPONS ENCYCLOPAEDIA

EDITORIAL STAFF
Luca Cristini, Paolo Crippa.

ACADEMIC STAFF
Enrico Acerbi, Massimiliano Afiero, Aldo Antonicelli, Ruggero Calò, Luigi Carretta, Flavio Chistè, Anna Cristini, Carlo Cucut, Salvo Fagone, Enrico Finazzer, Arturo Giusti, Björn Huber, Andrea Lombardi, Aymeric Lopez, Marco Lucchetti, Gabriele Malavoglia, Luigi Manes, Giovanni Maressi, Francesco Mattesini, Daniele Notaro, Péter Mujzer, Federico Peirani, Alberto Peruffo, Maurizio Raggi, Andrea Alberto Tallillo, Antonio Tallillo, Roberto Vela, Massimo Zorza.

PUBLISHED BY
Luca Cristini Editore (Soldiershop), via Orio, 35/4 - 24050 Zanica (BG) ITALY.

DISTRIBUTION BY
Soldiershop - www.soldiershop.com, Amazon, Ingram Spark, Berliner Zinnfigurem (D), LaFeltrinelli, Mondadori, Libera Editorial (Spain), Google book (eBook), Kobo, (eBoook), Apple Book (eBook).

PUBLISHING'S NOTES
None of unpublished images or text of our book may be reproduced in any format without the expressed written permission of Luca Cristini Editore (already Soldiershop.com) when not indicate as marked with license creative commons 3.0 or 4.0. Luca Cristini Editore has made every reasonable effort to locate, contact and acknowledge rights holders and to correctly apply terms and conditions to Content. Every effort has been made to trace the copyright of all the photographs. If there are unintentional omissions, please contact the publisher in writing at: info@soldiershop.com, who will correct all subsequent editions.

LICENSES COMMONS
This book may utilize part of material marked with license creative commons 3.0 or 4.0 (CC BY 4.0), (CC BY-ND 4.0), (CC BY-SA 4.0) or (CC0 1.0). We give appropriate attribution credit and indicate if change were made in the acknowledgments field. Our WTW books series utilize only fonts licensed under the SIL Open Font License or other free use license.

CONTRIBUTORS OF THIS VOLUME & ACKNOWLEDGEMENTS
We would like to thank the main contributors to this issue: above all the Associazione Modellisti Pumeneghesi AMP, headed by president Marino Paloschi, while the model vehicles are the work of Vezzoli Gianfelice, and Walter Ferrari. The profiles of the wagons are all by the author. The colouring of the photos is by Anna Cristini. Special thanks to national and/or private institutions such as: Army General Staff, State Archives, Bundesarchiv, Nara, Library of Congress, Wikipedia, USAF, Signal magazine, Cronache di guerra, Fronte di guerra, IWM, Australian War Museum, etc. A P.Crippa, A.Lopez, Péter Mujzer, L.Manes, C.Cucut, Tallillo archives. Model Victoria (www.modelvictoria.it) etc. for providing images or other items from their archives.

For a complete list of Soldiershop titles, or for every information please contact us on our website: www.soldiershop.com or www.cristinieditore.com. E-mail: info@soldiershop.com. Keep up to date on Facebook https://www.facebook.com/soldiershop.publishing

Title: **GERMAN EXPERIMENTAL TANKS - VOL. I** Code.: **TWE-032 EN**
Series by Luca Stefano Cristini
ISBN code: 9791255891925 First edition December 2024
THE WEAPONS ENCYCLOPAEDIA (SOLDIERSHOP) is a trademark of Luca Cristini Editore

THE WEAPONS ENCYCLOPÆDIA
TANK AIRCRAFT AFV SHIP ARTILLERY VEHICLES SECRET WEAPON

GERMAN EXPERIMENTAL TANKS VOL. I

DICKER MAX-GRILLE-LÖWE MAUS-VK 4501/02

LUCA STEFANO CRISTINI

BOOK SERIES FOR MODELERS & COLLECTORS

CONTENTS

Introduction 5
- The last German hope 5

10,5 cm K gepanzerte Selbstfahrlafette (Dicker Max) 9
- Description 9
- Operational roster 11

Geschützwagen Tiger 17/21 (Grille) 15
- History of the project 15
- The captured model 19

Panzer VII Löwe 21
- History and development 21
- Versions 23
- Propaganda weapon 25

Panzer VI Tiger (P) VK 4501 29
- Project development and operational history 29
- Technical specifications 31
- Modified versions of the Tiger (P) 35

Panzer VI Tiger VK 4502 Hinten & Vorne 37
- Project Progress 37
- The Porsche turret 39

Panzer VIII Maus 45
- Origins and Development 45
- Technical specifications 49
- Conclusions 51

German tank camouflage and insignia 52

Bibliography 58

▲ The experimental VK 4502 Hinten tank, made by Walter Ferrari from the Pumenengo (BG) modelling club.

INTRODUCTION

German supertanks were part of the **Wunderwaffen** (miracle weapons) projects, designed to win the war. Throughout the Second World War, advanced German design teams worked tirelessly on a bewildering variety of armoured vehicles of all shapes and sizes. This first volume deals with a sample of fascinating designs that were never mass-produced, but only as prototypes or in very small numbers. These were preferably heavy or even super-heavy tanks such as the VIII MAUS panzer, designed by Porsche, or others such as the VII Löwe panzer designed by Krupp engineers in various versions and studies; heavy fighters such as the Dicker Max or the mammoth Geschützwagen Tiger (Grille), followed later by the VK 4501/02 project tanks such as the Vorn and Hinten by Porsche and Krupp!
This study will then continue up to the so-called *E-Series* models that we will cover in the second volume along with other interesting designs.

■ THE LAST GERMAN HOPE

The **Wunderwaffen** were hypothetical super-weapons or secret weapons developed by the Third Reich. This term was introduced and spread by the German propaganda of the powerful minister Joseph Goebbels during the final stages of the Second World War. The aim of the propaganda was to create the illusion of imminent military technological superiority, capable of turning the tide of the conflict, which had now reached a clearly unfavourable situation for Germany.
Among the best known Wunderwaffen, and some of the few actually completed and used, are the Vergeltungswaffen ('revenge weapons'). However, most Wunderwaffen did not make it past the theoretical or prototype stage and, consequently, were never deployed in the field; when they were, it was often too late or in too small quantities to really influence the outcome of the war.
Examples of these weapons include the 'solar cannon' (Sonnengewehr), the German military nuclear project, and the Panzer VIII Maus tank and other supertanks that we discuss in this volume.

▲ Interior of the giant Krupp steelworks in Essen, working in the production of weapons.

Towards the end of the Second World War, the Third Reich engaged in a frantic race to develop new and powerful military technologies in the hope of reversing the inevitable defeat. Among the most ambitious inventions of the period, apart from rockets and ultra-modern aircraft, were the German experimental tanks, an area of military research that required huge economic, material and intellectual resources. These armoured vehicles, which were conceived with hitherto unseen technical specifications and dimensions, were designed to give the German army a strategic and psychological advantage over the Allies. However, most of them never made it beyond the prototype stage, and few were put to practical use on the battlefield.

The idea behind the experimental tanks was to create armoured vehicles with unprecedented firepower and endurance, capable of taking on the strongest enemy lines and effectively countering the increasingly advanced and numerous armoured forces of the Allies and the Soviet Union.

German designers worked on a variety of prototypes, from heavy tanks such as the Panzer VIII Maus and the E-100 to so-called 'super tanks' and 'super-heavy tanks', designed to outgun any known Allied armament. These vehicles, with their mammoth dimensions and colossal weight, were to possess almost impenetrable armour and lethal firepower, often through the integration of high-calibre anti-tank guns. The Panzer VIII Maus, for example, was a veritable colossus: weighing over 180 tonnes, it was the heaviest tank ever built. Designed by Ferdinand Porsche, this vehicle was supposed to be virtually immune to conventional weapons, thanks to its massive armour and a powerful 128 mm cannon. However, its impressiveness also turned out to be its greatest limitation: the Maus was extremely slow and virtually incapable of crossing bridges or moving smoothly in urban or rugged environments. Apart from two prototypes, the Maus never entered large-scale production, as the military and logistical situation in Germany in 1944-1945 did not allow for the implementation of such complex and expensive vehicles.

▲ The prototype of one of the parents of the famous Tiger I. This is Porsche's Panzerkampfwagen VI Tiger (P) VK4501, photographed here with the first dummy turret without gun.

▲ Nice view of a Jagdtiger 305 tank destroyer entering with its long gun barrel into the cockpit of the Grille parked right in front. These were two truly mammoth tanks!

▲ Porsche would probably prefer to forget that, during the World War, it was, through its founder Ferdinand Porsche, Hitler's point of contact and associate and contributed in no small measure to the development of new weapons.

▲ Of the two Dicker Maxes both used on the Russian front, one caught fire and was destroyed; the second had a longer life. Here we see probably its last photo, taken near Stalingrad in February 1942, being examined by a Soviet soldier. Note the typical German tracing of successes against enemy tanks drawn on the gun barrel. Apparently, this second model also took the name 'Brummbar'.

At the same time, other models were being developed such as the E-100, conceived as a more manoeuvrable and simplified version of the Maus. The E-100 was part of the *Entwicklungsserie* project, a series of standardised tanks that were to gradually replace the entire German armoured fleet, allowing for greater flexibility in production and maintenance. This project, although highly innovative, remained at an early stage, also hampered by the chronic lack of resources and the urgent need to defend Germany's borders from Allied armies.

In addition to armoured behemoths, German designers also explored unconventional solutions, such as rocket-propelled tanks and extremely light and fast crawlers, designed for reconnaissance operations or sudden attacks. These ideas, although innovative, remained largely theoretical and did not make it past the test phase. The enormous efforts and hopes pinned on the experimental tanks reflected German desperation, but also the high level of engineering and creativity that characterised German military technology at the time.

However, by the end of the war, most of these prototypes lay unfinished or abandoned in production plants, while the few completed examples were quickly studied and taken over by the Allies, fascinated by what appeared to be the mad ambition to build 'invincible' armoured vehicles. The legacy of these experimental tanks was also felt after the war: German designs and technical solutions inspired, in part, the evolution of modern tanks. Despite the fact that most of them never reached the front, these experimental vehicles embodied the Third Reich's final attempt to change the course of the war with illusory technological superiority, yet left an indelible mark on the history of armoured forces.

10.5 CM K GEPANZERTE SELBSTFAHRLAFETTE "DICKER MAX"

The 10.5 cm Kanone (gepanzerte Selbstfahrlafette), better known by the nickname Dicker Max, abbreviated to 10.5 cm K (gp.Sfl) (translatable into Italian as '10.5 cm armoured self-propelled cannon'), was a prototype self-propelled artillery gun developed by German engineers. Initially conceived and designed as an anti-bunker weapon suitable for breaking through the Maginot Line, known as the Schartenbrecher, after the surrender of France it was reconsidered for use as a heavy tank destroyer on the Eastern Front.

In 1939, Krupp began the development of a vehicle capable of hitting enemy fortifications while remaining safe from retaliatory fire. After the swift French defeat, however, this requirement was no longer met, and the design was therefore re-adapted to the role of a heavy tank destroyer. Two prototypes were ordered, completed in January 1941 and presented to Hitler on 31 March. If the tests were positive, Krupp planned to start series production in the spring of 1942.

In the development phase, the vehicle was called 10 cm K (Pz.Sfl.IVa), and received its official name of 10.5 cm K (gp.Sfl.) on 13 August 1941. Among the troops, it was nicknamed 'Dicker Max' (Max the Fat).

DESCRIPTION

The Dicker Max was built using the modified hull of the Panzerkampfwagen IV Ausf. E, without turret and equipped with an open casemate for the gun. The front plate was 50 mm thick hardened steel, inclined at 15° from vertical, while the side armour was 20 mm. A distinctive feature of the vehicle was the casemate protecting the rear fighting compartment. The 26 on-board ammunition was located in special armoured containers. The pilot's seat was located to the front left, with a dummy seat to the right.

The cannon was also designed to counter enemy armoured vehicles, but had a range of only 8° left and right, and an elevation between -15° and +10°. A muzzle brake was introduced on the barrel to reduce recoil and a recoil pad to block the barrel when moving. For close-range defence, the crew had three machine guns and 576 rounds. The aimer used a Selbstfahrlafetten-Zielfernrohr 1 (Sfl.Z.F. 1) optic, and the tank leader had a binocular periscope on a rotating arm at his disposal.

▲ The 10.5 cm K (gp.Sfl.) used a standard Panzer IV suspension. Although not immune to various technical imperfections, the vehicle was simple and easy to maintain.

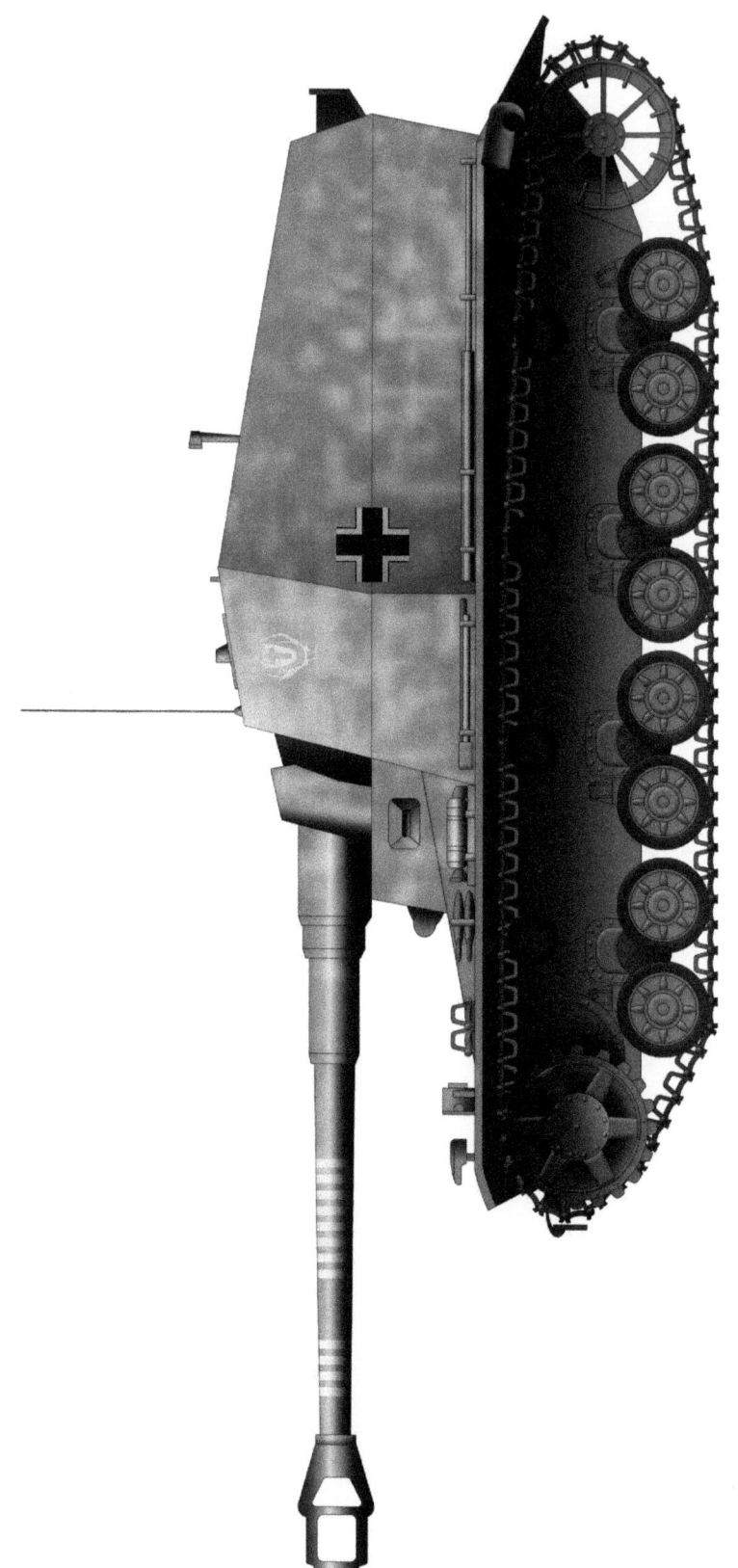

10 cm Kanone Panzer Selbstfahrlafette IVa, better known by the nickname Dicker Max (Fat Max) belonging to Panzerjäger-Abteilung 521 winter version, Russian Eastern Front. Summer 1942.

The V-12 Maybach HL120 engine of the Panzer IV was replaced with a lighter V-6 Maybach HL66P. The production vehicles were to receive the suspension system of the Panzer III, which ensured greater manoeuvrability due to a shorter track, lower wheel resistance, softer suspension and greater shock absorber travel.

OPERATIONAL ROSTER

Made in only two prototypes, the Dicker Max ended up assigned to Panzerjäger-Abteilung 521 during Operation Barbarossa. One of the two prototypes accidentally caught fire, with the ammunition explosion causing its complete destruction, while the other successfully participated in combat until late 1941. This second prototype was then modified by Krupp in the first half of 1942 on the basis of field experience and was sent back into service to participate in the Blaue Operation. There are no operational mentions of the prototype in the battalion reports between November and December.

A report dated 26 July 1941 stated: 'This self-propelled vehicle is not manoeuvrable enough for use in a forward-deployed unit. The limited pivoting forces the entire vehicle to rotate to aim at targets, a time-consuming operation, especially in rough terrain, due to the weight and low engine power. In addition, the distribution of the armour - reinforced at the front but only 50 mm thick at the rear - makes the vehicle very vulnerable at the flanks and rear. It is effective in supporting frontal infantry attacks with direct fire, but the dust raised by the cannon makes it impossible to observe the effect of the shots. A side observation post or an alternative cannon would be required. Due to its size, limited mobility and dust raised by the gun, it is only suitable for firing explosive grenades with indirect fire. ... In its assigned roles - direct attack against bunkers and engagement of heavy tanks - the vehicle has demonstrated adequate penetration capabilities, without significant engine and transmission problems, although the steering brakes are overloaded, with frequent repairs required."

DATA SHEET 10,5 CM KANONE (GEPANZERTE SELBSTFAHRLAFETTE)	
Designation	Dicker Max
Lenght	747 cm
Width	286 cm
Height	253 cm
Setting date	199-1941
Weight in combat order	22 t
Crew	5 (commander, driver, 2 servants and gunner)
Engine	Maybach HL 66 P, 6 cylinders, water-cooled, 6.6 l. 180 hp
Maximum speed	27 km/h on road 17 km/h off road
Autonomy	170 km on road, 120 off road
Elevation	-15° + 10°
Armouring	From 10 o 50mm
Armament	1 x 10.5 L/52 gun 1 MP 40 9mm machine gun
Production	2

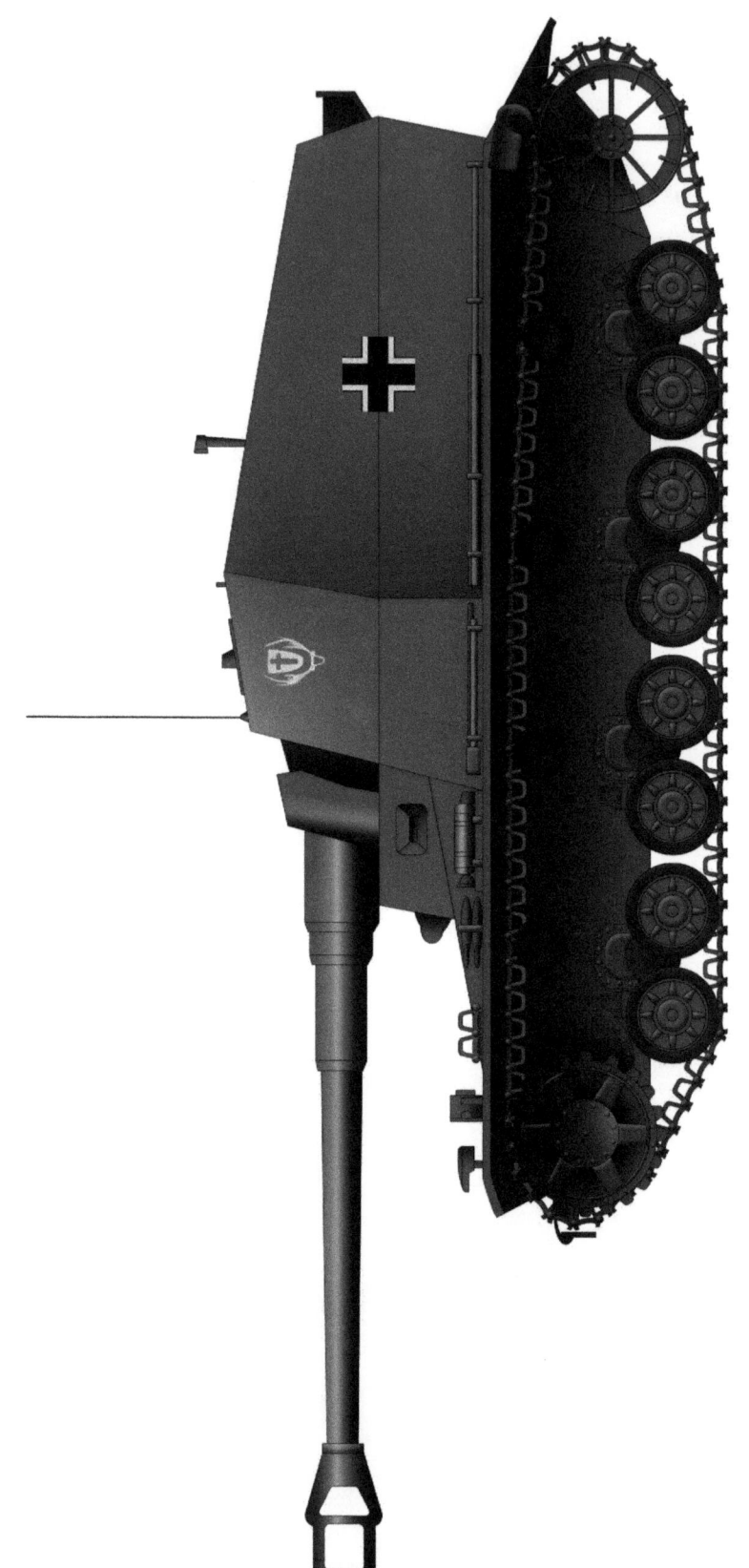

Tank 10 cm Kanone Panzer Selbstfahrlafette IVa, better known by the nickname Dicker Max (Fat Max) in the typical feldgrau colour. Russians 1941.

▲ Images of a model of the experimental Dicker Max wagon made by Vezzoli Gianfelice, a member of the Pumenengo (BG) modelling club by kind permission.

GERMAN EXPERIMENTAL TANKS VOL. I

▲ Beautiful side view of the 10.5 cm K (gp.Sfl.) engaged in Russia within Panzerjäger-Abteilung 521. A Panzer II is visible behind it.

▲ The vehicle required a crew of five soldiers; four (commander, gunner and two servants) were housed in the rear casemate, the pilot in his cramped front corner.

GESCHÜTZWAGEN TIGER – GRILLE 17/21

The Geschützwagen Tiger (GW Tiger) known as the Grille was a German World War II self-propelled gunship that never entered service. The idea came in May 1942, to the German company Krupp, which proposed the construction of a new armoured self-propelled vehicle based on components of the existing Panzerkampfwagen VI Tiger.

"Geschützwagen' literally means 'cannon vehicle' in German, but a more accurate description would be 'mobile gun carriage'. This car was in fact designed to transport various weapons, with a modern modular approach. The vehicle was also called a 'Grille', which means 'cricket' in German.

Although the design was derived from the Tiger chassis, the prototype was significantly modified to suit this new purpose. The vehicle designed was to be able to mount two types of cannon.

These could be either the 17 cm Kanone K72 (Sf) cannon or the 21 cm Mörser 18/1 short-barreled howitzer, which used the same mounting system; the former model would be called the Grille 17, while the latter Grille 21.

Krupp's proposal was officially presented on 6 May 1942 to the Wa Prüf 4 artillery division of the German High Command, which gave the go-ahead for the project to build a prototype with an initial completion date of 1 November 1942. The vehicle was required to be able to rotate 360 degrees to allow it to also be used in coastal defence.

■ PROJECT HISTORY

A later model, the GW Tiger Geschutzwagen, was conceived in June 1942, when it was decided to develop a heavy artillery piece mounted on an extended Tiger II chassis. The prototype was tested shortly before the end of the war, but as Germany was close to surrendering, the vehicle never entered service and was captured by the Allies. The elongated chassis of the Grille 17/21 was much longer than that of the standard Tiger, and this created major problems for the designers in Essen. Krupp eventually had to find creative solutions to accommodate the guns, which were too heavy for a traditional turret.

In January 1943, the vehicle, based on the Tiger Ausf B model, was officially requested. It was planned that the gun would have a 360° rotation via a turntable, but in the end a simpler solution was chosen.

▲ The only prototype captured as evidence of the Grille's design. It was found by US Third Army men at the Henschel test centre in Haustenbeck, along with other German vehicles.

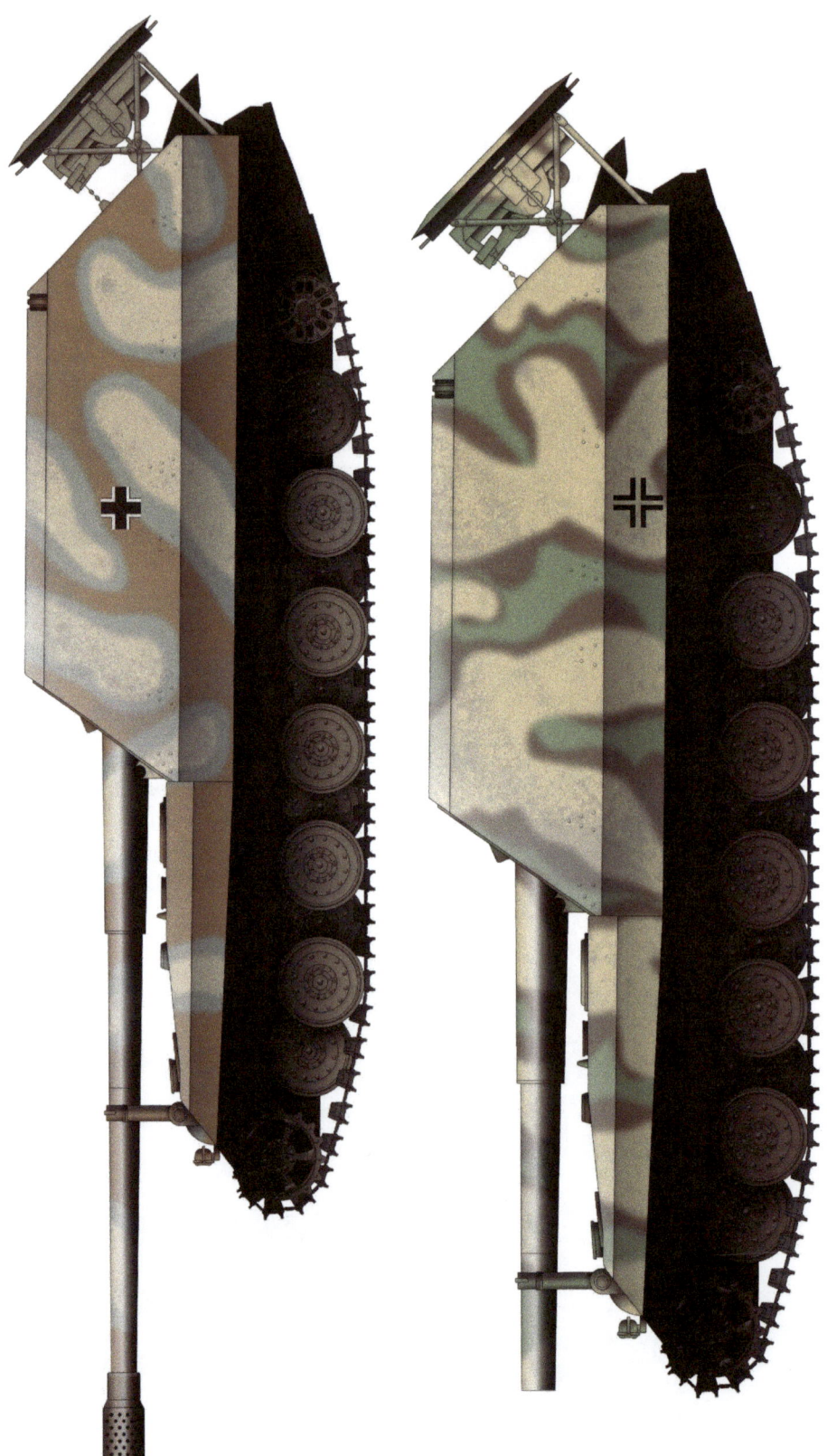

Above: Tank Geschützwagen Tiger 17cm K72 (Grille)
Below: Geschützwagen Tiger 21cm Mörser 18-1 tank

▲ Impressive picture of the interior of the Grille found in Haustenbeck. The presence of the three American soldiers gives a good idea of the size of this armoured giant.

DATA SHEET - GESCHÜTZWAGEN TIGER 17CM K72 (GRILLE)	
Designation	Grille
Lenght	1300 cm
Width	327 cm
Height	315 cm
Setting date	June 1942
Weight in combat order	from 58 to 64 t
Crew	7/8 (commander, driver and 6 gunners)
Engine	Maybach HL 230P30 700 cv
Maximum speed	35 km/h on road 18 km/h off road
Autonomy	250 km on road, 120 off road
Producer	Krupp by Essen
Armouring	From 16 to 30mm
Armament	1 17 cm K72 L/50 gun or 21 cm M18/1 L 31 m mortar or 420 mm mortar 1 7.92 mm machine gun
Production	1 specimen/prototype (partial) from Krupp

▲ Images of a model of the experimental Geschützwagen Tiger (GW Tiger) tank known as the Grille, made by Vezzoli Gianfelice, a member of the Pumenengo (BG) modelling club, courtesy of courtesy of Vezzoli.

For this purpose, a complex circular plate was built and carried on the back of the vehicle; this would be placed on the ground during use and the vehicle would then be positioned on top of it to allow the vehicle and consequently the gun to rotate.

Another requirement of the German army was to make the cannons detachable. To do this, the vehicle would then have to back up to the plate to slide the cannon out and mount it, thus allowing full rotation even for coastal use. However, in 1944 this requirement was removed by direct order of Heinrich Himmler.

Initially, the vehicle was to be equipped with relatively light armour of 30 mm at the front and 16 mm at the sides. In November 1942, it was decided to use carbon steel, with 50 mm at the front and 30 mm at the sides and rear, which greatly increased the overall weight. The planned completion in November 1942 was continually delayed. The lack of necessary components continued so long that the prototype was only finished in the summer of 1944.

The Allied Air Force meanwhile bombed the Krupp factory in Essen on a daily basis, further complicating the project. The High Command finally halted the project in 1945, as resources were scarce and it was preferred to allocate them to other weapons.

A British report from 1945 indicated that the planned crew was seven to eight people. The armament was to be loaded manually, with some crew and ammunition transported on an 18-ton auxiliary half-track.

The first prototype was sent to Sennelager well behind schedule for testing only in the latter stages of the war. Due to difficulties in the production of conventional heavy artillery, an order was issued in January 1945 to make heavy smoothbore mortars capable of launching long-distance fin-stabilised projectiles. Krupp and Škoda competed for the project, and Škoda produced a prototype of the 30.5 cm Granat Werfer (Gr. W.) mortar in early April 1945. A 42 cm Gr. W. mortar was also being developed. These mortars automatically returned to an elevation angle of 40° for reloading. The Grille, designed to mount this weapon, would have four hydraulic jacks to stabilise during firing. But by this time the situation had become untenable for Germany, and the Grille and its various weapon options remained just an interesting hypothesis.

■ THE CAPTURED MODEL

The prototype of the Grille 17/21 was found almost intact and without a mounted gun at the Henschel test centre in Haustenbeck. The vehicle was 'parked' next to a King Tiger with initial turret, a Panther and a Jagdtiger. It was the US Third Army that captured these vehicles and the Grille with the necessary 17 cm cannon. No other frames or a 21 cm Mörser were found.

▲ Alongside the Grille prototype, the barrel of the 17 cm K72 L/50 gun was also found.

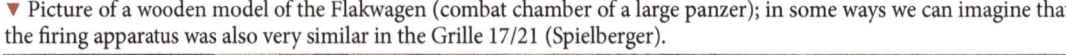

▲ Another image of the captured prototype of the Grille on page 15, this time viewed from the rear.
▼ Picture of a wooden model of the Flakwagen (combat chamber of a large panzer); in some ways we can imagine that the firing apparatus was also very similar in the Grille 17/21 (Spielberger).

PANZER VII LÖWE

The Panzer VII Löwe (lion), short for Panzerkampfwagen VII Löwe, was an articulated super-heavy tank design developed by Nazi Germany in the middle of World War II. Conceived in early 1942 to counter large Soviet tanks, the Panzer VII Löwe was proposed in at least three main versions and some minor variants, but never gained final approval from the military leadership. There were two versions considered most promising, a 'light' (leichte) and a 'heavy' (schwere), but neither made it to the prototype stage.

HISTORY AND DEVELOPMENT

On 22 June 1941, with the start of Operation Barbarossa, Germany sought to quickly defeat the Soviet Union. However, the tank battles that followed highlighted the superiority, or at least the robustness, of Soviet armoured vehicles, such as the KV-1, compared to the Panzer IV, the most advanced then available to the German army. A number of captured Soviet tanks were studied by German engineers, and Krupp began designing a super-heavy tank to deal with them effectively.

This led to November 1941, when the preliminary requirements for the new tank were established: a frontal armour thickness of 140 mm and side armour thickness of 100 mm, with an estimated weight of around 90 tonnes. A 1,000-horsepower Daimler-Benz engine, traditionally used on the Kriegsmarine's Schnellboote, was chosen to ensure a speed of around 44 km/h. The planned crew consisted of five members, three of them in the turret and two in the hull. In early 1942, Krupp was commissioned to develop the Panzer VII, identified as VK 7201 and named 'Löwe' (lion), based on the VK7001 design and using components from the Panzer VI Tiger II to simplify production.

Of the first two versions of the Löwe, one 76-tonne and one 90-tonne, it was the heavier one that was preferred by Hitler for further development. However, between February and May 1942, no less than six design variants were examined, without any being approved. Meanwhile, on 6 March 1942, the army requested new specifications for an even heavier tank, suspending the Löwe project in July to concentrate on the Panzer Maus project (which we will discuss later).

▲ Experimental tank Pz.Kpfw VII Löwe (leichte, light version) with 150 mm L/40 gun.

Experimental tank Pz.Kpfw VII Löwe (Schwerer heavy version) with 150 mm L/40 gun.

VERSIONS

Two alternatives were mainly developed, a light one with a 76-tonne rear turret and 100 mm frontal armour, and a heavy one with 90 tonnes and 120 mm armour. Both were armed with a 105 mm L/70 cannon and an MG34 coaxial machine gun.

Leichter Löwe (Light Version): This version of the Löwe had a turret mounted off-centre at the rear of the hull, equipped with a 105 mm cannon and a coaxial machine gun. It had 100 mm frontal armour and an estimated weight of 76 tonnes, allowing it to reach speeds of 27 km/h. However, no prototype was ever built.

Schwerer Löwe (Heavy Version): The heavy version had 120 mm frontal armour and a turret in the centre of the hull. While keeping the armament unchanged, the weight increased to 90 tonnes, reducing the maximum speed to 23 km/h. Hitler always preferred this heavy variant. Later, at the Führer's own request, a version armed with the 150 mm KwK 44 L/38 cannon and 140 mm frontal armour, with wide tracks for better mobility, and an engine boosted to reach 30 km/h was proposed, but even this version never went into production, and towards the end of 1942 the Löwe project, by then in competition with Porsche's Maus, was finally abandoned.

Third Version: In late 1942, during the development of the Tiger II, Colonel Fichtner commissioned Henschel & Sohn to rework the Löwe's design. This new version, still based on the Schwerer's central turret, was equipped with a lighter 88 mm KwK 43 cannon, 140 mm front armour, and an 800 hp Maybach HL 230 PL engine. With a total weight of 90 tonnes, it could have reached a speed of around 35 km/h, but it too remained on paper and the project was eventually abandoned.

DATA SHEET - PANZER VII LÖWE (Schwerer)	
Designation	Löwe (lion)
Lenght	774 cm
Width	380 cm
Height	308 cm
Setting date	November 1941- July 1942
Weight in combat order	90 t (76 t the Leichte)
Crew	5 (commander, driver, 1 radio operator and 2 gunners)
Engine	Maybach HL 230PL 12-cylinder 800 hp
Maximum speed	35 km/h on road 25 km/h off road
Autonomy	160 km on road, 80 off road
Producer	Krupp by Essen
Armouring	From 40 to 180mm
Armament	1 KwK 43 105mm gun 1 MG 34 7.92 mm machine gun
Production	none

Two more pictures of the experimental tank Pz.Kpfw VII Löwe (Schwerer heavy version) with 150 mm L/40 gun in different camo versions.

PROPAGANDA WEAPON

As early as 1941, Germany studied the development of super-heavy tanks, vehicles that, although of dubious tactical utility and complicated to produce, were highly effective as propaganda tools. Propaganda Minister Joseph Goebbels, a master at such things, promoted it as one of the so-called Wunderwaffen.

▲ Images of a model of the experimental Pz.Kpfw VII Löwe (Leichte light version), made by Vezzoli Gianfelice, a member of the Pumenengo (BG) modelling club, courtesy of the Pumenengo (BG) modelling club.

Experimental tank Pz.Kpfw VII Löwe (leichte light version) with 150 mm L/40 gun.

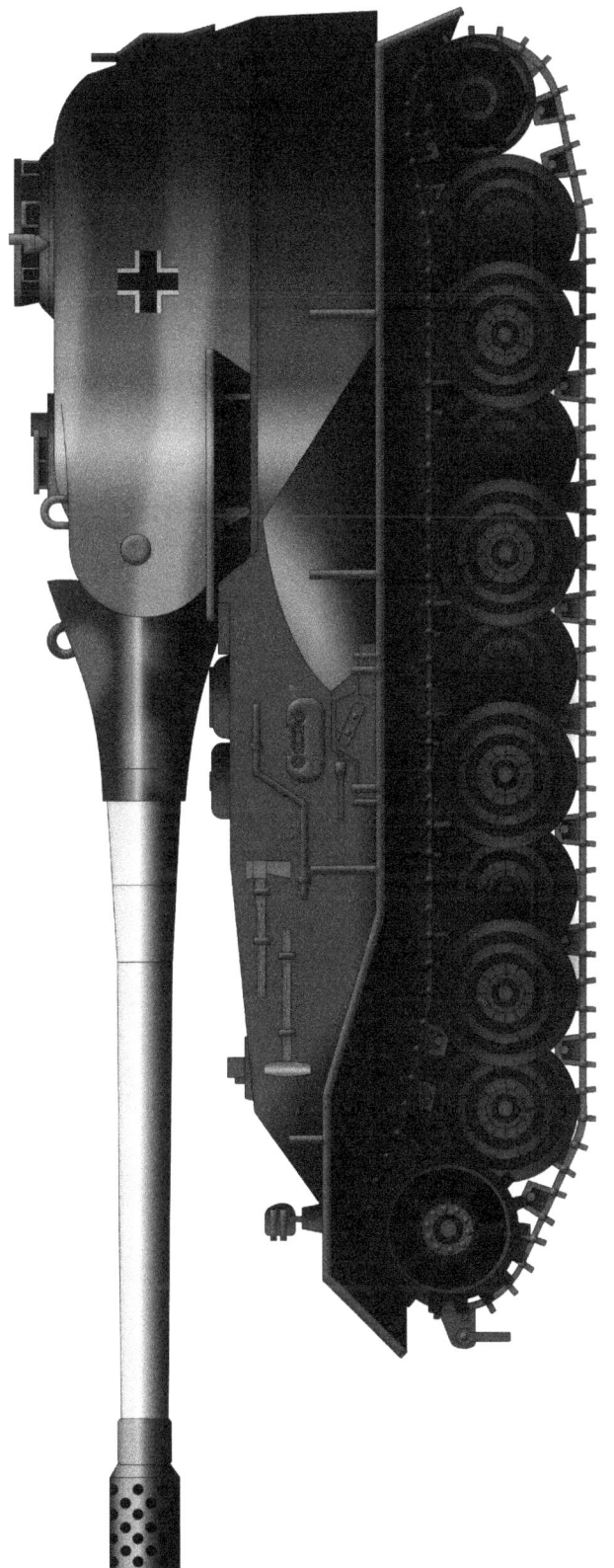

Experimental tank Pz.Kpfw VII Löwe (leichte light version) with 150 mm L/40 gun.

▲ Images of a model of the experimental Pz.Kpfw VII Löwe (Leichte light version), made by Vezzoli Gianfelice, a member of the Pumenengo (BG) modelling club, courtesy of the Pumenengo (BG) modelling club.

PANZER VI TIGER (P) VK 4501

THE MISSED BROTHER OF THE LEGENDARY TIGER I

The Panzer VI Tiger (P), officially named Panzerkampfwagen VI Tiger (P) and also known as VK 4501(P), was a heavy tank developed in Germany during World War II. This armoured vehicle was, like many others, created to counter T-34 tanks and other armoured vehicles of the Red Army. It was designed by engineer Ferdinand Porsche, who adopted an innovative drive solution based on electric motors. However, during testing, the vehicle revealed numerous mechanical problems, making it unsuitable for operational use. This eventually led to a lack of interest, resulting in the production of only five examples, of which only one was sent to the Eastern Front, while the others were used for training at the Döllersheim military base in Austria. However, the VK 4501(P) was credited with providing the basis for the later development of the Elefant heavy fighter.

PROJECT DEVELOPMENT AND OPERATIONAL HISTORY

Starting in 1937, the German high command began the search for a more heavily armed and armoured replacement for the Panzer IV, with the aim of countering the British and French heavy tanks encountered during the French campaign in 1940. On 26 May 1941, during a meeting dedicated to the selection of new armaments, Hitler commissioned Ferdinand Porsche and the managers of Henschel & Sohn to design a 45-tonne heavy tank, armed with the land-based version of the famous FlaK 88 anti-aircraft gun. As a result of this double assignment, Porsche models were given the suffix (P), and Henschel models the suffix (H).

DATA SHEET - PANZER VI TIGER (P) VK 4501	
Type	Heavy tank
Lenght	670 cm
Width	338 cm
Height	280 cm
Setting date	First test: July 1942
Weight in combat order	58 t
Crew	5 (commander, driver, 1 radio operator, servant and gunner)
Engine	Porsche Type 101/1 10-cylinder, petrol and water-cooled
Maximum speed	35 km/h on road 20 km/h off road
Autonomy	110 km on road, 50 off road
Producer	Porsche and Henschel & Sohn
Armouring	From 60 to 100mm
Armament	1 KwK 36 88 mm gun 1 or 2 MG 34 7.92 mm machine guns
Production	about 6 to 10

Prototype of the Versuchskraftfahrzeug (VK) 45.01(P) experimental tank with dummy turret.

The ambitious new *Tigerprogramm* was almost immediately joined by Krupp, which won the contract to supply the turrets and armament. Porsche's design, based on the VK 3001(P), was completed in July 1942, but proved to be problematic and defective during testing: in particular, the dual petrol-engine/electric drive system proved to be delicate, requiring frequent maintenance. As a result, the Henschel-designed tank successfully passed the tests, and in October 1942 the verdict became final and the prototype went into production, becoming the famous and feared Panzer VI Tiger I, perhaps the most famous of German tanks.

At the end of the project, Nibelungenwerke therefore only produced five units of the Tiger (P), among others, as mentioned above, with components supplied by Krupp, with hull numbers between 150001 and 150010. Porsche, despite the absence of an official order, had nevertheless started production in the confidence that the design would later be approved by Hitler. Of all these examples, of the two manufacturers, only one was later adapted as a command tank, equipped with upgraded armour and a Maybach engine and sent to the Eastern Front, in the ranks of the schwere Panzerjäger Abteilung 653, where it served until its destruction in July 1944.

TECHNICAL SPECIFICATIONS

The propulsion system was based on two petrol-powered Porsche Type 101/1 engines with components similar to the VK 3001(P) that activated electric generators for independent motors on each track. The vehicle was equipped with wide tracks to better distribute the weight and facilitate movement over soft terrain, but the size and weight of the vehicle limited its manoeuvrability.
However, this configuration was very inefficient and prone to frequent breakdowns.
The vehicle's passive defence was equipped with strong armour. The front hull was protected with 80-100 mm of armour, with additional protection on the turret mantle up to 145 mm.
As for armament, this Tiger was equipped with an 88 mm KwK 36 cannon, capable of penetrating thick armour at various distances, and a 7.92 mm MG 34 machine gun. It carried up to 80 shells for the cannon

▲ The prototype of the Panzerkampfwagen VI Tiger (P) VK4501 equipped with a dummy turret.

Experimental tank Pz.Kpfw VI Tiger (P) - Panzerbefehlswagen derived from the protype with the addition of the turret and the 88 mm piece.

▲▼ Several rare and interesting pictures of the only Panzerkampfwagen VI Tiger (P) tank that entered action, deployed on the Eastern Front, in the ranks of the schwere Panzerjäger Abteilung 653, where it served until its destruction in July 1944.

Experimental tank Pz.Kpfw VI Tiger (P) - Panzerbefehlswagen used by the Pnzer. Jag. Abt. 653 on the Oriental front until the summer of 1944.

and over 4,300 rounds of ammunition for the machine gun.

The presence or absence of a second machine gun is unclear. The crew consisted of five members: in the turret were the commander, gunner and loader; in the hull sat the pilot on the left and the gunner on the right.

Weighing around 60 tonnes, it reached a maximum speed of 35 km/h on the road. On rough terrain, the speed dropped to 8-10 km/h, severely limiting operational effectiveness.

MODIFIED VERSIONS OF THE TIGER (P)

Rammtiger (P)

On 22 November 1942, Hitler authorised the creation of a prototype called the Rammtiger (P), also known as the 'Tiger-Aircraft'. This armoured vehicle was designed to break down obstacles and barricades, a necessity that emerged during the Battle of Stalingrad, where ruins and barricades erected by the Soviets had often blocked the advance of German armoured vehicles. On 7 December 1942, Porsche completed the plans, which involved fitting the chassis with an aerodynamic profile to slide debris to the sides. The vehicle was fitted with a ploughshare-like prow and retained a casemate housing for an MG 34 or MG 42 machine gun. The armour was to be 30 mm thick on all sides, with the roof reinforced to 50 mm. The planned dimensions were 8.25 metres long, 3.6 metres wide and 2.55 metres high. On 5 January 1943, Hitler decided to convert three Tiger (P) to the new model, and the corresponding superstructures were ready in May 1943. By August, three Rammtiger were completed, but it is unlikely that they were ever used: in all likelihood, they remained in the warehouses of the Nibelungenwerke.

Bergepanzer Tiger (P)

Between August and September 1943, three of the five Tigers (P) in Döllersheim were converted into rescue tanks, taking the name 'Bergepanzer Tiger (P)'. The Nibelungenwerke took care of the conversion: the new vehicle weighed 60 tonnes, measured about 8 metres in length and 1.97 metres in height, as a low superstructure with a 7.92 mm MG 42 machine gun on the right side was mounted in place of the turret. The two unreliable Porsche engines were replaced with 12-cylinder V-shaped Maybach HL 120 TRM

▲ The prototype of the Panzerkampfwagen VI Tiger (P) VK4501 during the first tests.

engines, each capable of developing 272 horsepower at 2800 rpm. These petrol-powered, liquid-cooled engines guaranteed a range of 150 kilometres on the road and around 90 kilometres off-road thanks to a 950-litre fuel tank. The crew, increased to six members, could use two radios, a FuG 2 and a FuG 5. The armour was increased to 200 mm, with the minimum thickness increasing from 20 to 30 mm.

The Ferdinand/Elefant

In September 1942, given the advanced state of the works, the idea of using the ninety Tiger (P) hulls that had just been delivered to set up two heavy tank battalions (schwere Panzer-Abteilung) to be sent to Tunisia was considered, but technical problems made the plan unfeasible. It was then proposed to equip the hulls with 150 or 170 mm howitzers, or 210 mm mortars, but none of these plans were realised. In fact, on 22 September, it was decided instead to transform the Tiger (P) into self-propelled assault vehicles armed with an 88 mm PaK 43/2 L/71 gun. The new vehicle, with upgraded frontal armour and a casemate-mounted cannon, was named 'Ferdinand' in honour of Dr Porsche, but was later renamed 'Elefant' and was a rather successful vehicle!

▲▼ Two more pictures of the Panzerkampfwagen VI Tiger (P) tank in service on the Eastern Front. Above he is seen crammed onto the express train carriage, and to the side in fine profile with all the members of his Crew. Russia, spring 1944.

PANZER VI TIGER VK 4502 HINTEN & VORNE

The VK 45.02 (P) was the official designation for an unsuccessful heavy tank project designed by Ferdinand Porsche in Nazi Germany during World War II to compete with Henschel's design.
Unlike the earlier VK 45.01 (P) project, none of the prototypes were produced and tested. However, the design work became important because, from the first collaboration with Krupp, the combat turret planned for this vehicle with a long 8.8 cm KwK L/71 was actually produced and used on the first fifty Panzerkampfwagen VI Tiger IIs.
Development of this vehicle began in April 1942, with two design variants (Ausf. A and Ausf. B) incorporating different features. The Krupp company received an order for the construction of 50 turrets at the same time. However, the prototype hull for them was never produced. The turrets were therefore mounted on the first Tiger IIs that were to be armed with a KwK L/71 gun, like its Henschel counterpart.

■ PROJECT PROGRESS

After the VK 45.01 (P) failed to win the contract, Ferdinand Porsche tirelessly began looking for ways to improve the design for a future version. Based on the latest Allied tank designs, however, it was clear that simply increasing the armour of the VK 45.01 (P) would not be enough to keep his tank competitive. It had to have both more weight and greater manoeuvrability. What initially began as a single vehicle, dubbed 'Typ 180', later developed into a series of five different vehicles, which required the development of two different hull configurations: the Hinten with its turret housed on the rear and named Typ 181and the Vorne with its turret on the front/centre, named Typ 180. The overall design known as the VK 45.02 (P), also had both an electric and hydraulic drive system and as many as four different engines. The

DATA SHEET - PANZER VI TIGER (P) VK 4502	
Tipo	Heavy tank
Lenght	1070 cm including gun barrel
Width	332 cm
Height	295 cm
Setting date	April 1942
Weight in combat order	56/63 t
Crew	5 (commander, driver, 1 radio operator, servant and gunner)
Engine	2 Porsche type 101/3, 680 CV (500 kW; 670 CV)
Maximum speed	38 km/h on road 20 km/h off road
Autonomy	unknown
Producer	Porsche
Armouring	From 70 to 120mm
Armament	1 KwK 43 88 mm gun 2 MG 34 7.92 mm machine guns
Production	None (but used 50 Porsche turrets)

Experimental tank Pz.Kpfw VI Tiger (P) - VK 4502 'Vorne'.

designation used for the project during the Second World War in the development plans of the German war industry and the Army Weapons Office was descriptive in nature and should be read as follows: 'VK' for 'test project', the '45' relates to the weight in tonnes, while the '01, 2 etc' for the first or second of the different variants. The names, on the other hand, from the German Vorne and Hinten meant front and rear respectively. However, the prototype hull was never produced.

■ THE PORSCHE TURRET

The situation was different for the combat turret designed and developed by Krupp for this Porsche project for this new tank. Porsche and Krupp had already worked closely together on the development of the previous VK 45.01 (P) and this work continued. The aim was to mount an 8.8-cm tank gun with greater penetration power. This could not be mounted on the Tiger I chassis, even though it was Adolf Hitler's express wish that the heavy and famous German tank be armed with this weapon.

Krupp and Porsche agreed on a turret that had a relatively narrow front for the gun mantle and widened towards the sides to the width of the turret swivel ring in a curved plate. To compensate for the weight of the gun and create sufficient space for the return of the gun, the rear of the turret protruded considerably beyond the edge of the turret's rotating ring. In the basic concept, ammunition was stored in this rear part of the turret. While the Porsche development team continued to work on the vehicle hull, development work at Krupp was soon completed and production of the turrets began. After the Army Weapons Office had decided on Henschel's competitor model, the VK 45.03 (H), and ascertained that production of the new turrets for this model had not yet begun. Considering the turrets already produced for the Porsche project, these beautiful fighting turrets, which have since been called Porsche turrets to distinguish them, ended up being mounted on the first 50 chassis of the new Panzerkampfwagen VI Tiger II main battle tank and delivered to the heavy tank divisions.

▲ The only existing example of a 'Royal Tiger' Type 180 with a 'Porsche' dome is now preserved at the Tank Museum in Bovington, UK. Courtesy by Toshonenov wiki cc1.

Experimental tank Pz.Kpfw VI Tiger (P) - VK 4502 'Vorne' camo version.

▲ Images of a model of the experimental VK 4502 Hinten tank, made by Walter Ferrari, a member of the Pumenengo (BG) modelling club by kind permission.

Experimental tank Pz.Kpfw VI Tiger (P) - VK 4502 'Hinten' camo version.

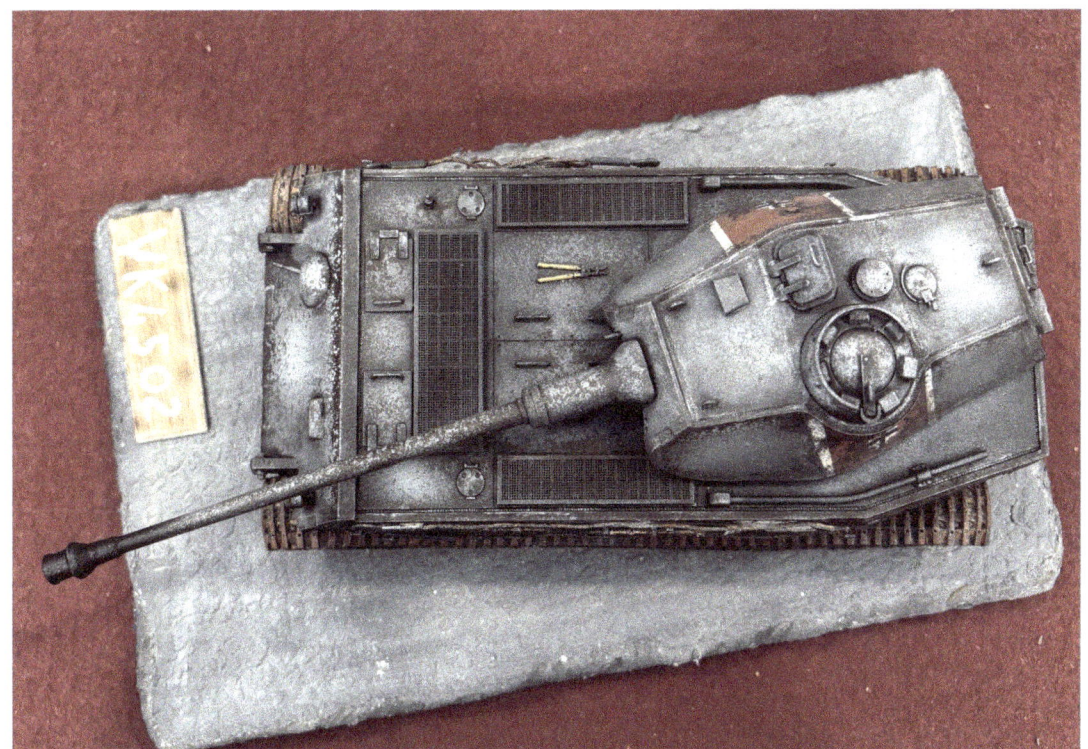

▲▼ Images of a model of the experimental VK 4502 Hinten wagon, made by Walter Ferrari, a member of the Pumenengo (BG) modelling club by kind permission.

GERMAN EXPERIMENTAL TANKS VOL. I

Experimental tank Pz.Kpfw VI Tiger (P) - VK 4502 'Hinten' 2nd camo version.

PANZER VIII MAUS

THE PANZERKAMPFWAGEN VIII 'MAUS': THE WEHRMACHT'S SUPER-HEAVY TANK

The Panzerkampfwagen VIII 'Maus' (mouse) was a super-heavy tank developed for the Wehrmacht during the Second World War. The creators, including high-ranking engineers and politicians, imagined that this vehicle would dominate the battlefield, outclassing any opponent. An effective Wunderwaffen in essence! However, production difficulties, attacks and attacks on the factories and the unfolding conflict prevented mass production. By the end of 1944, despite all efforts, only two prototypes were completed, only one of which was equipped with a turret. They received the following Porsche designations: tank 205, with the first completed example bearing the number 205/1 and the second 205/2.

■ ORIGINS AND DEVELOPMENT

A central role in the development of the project was played by the Tank Commission, created in 1939 under the direction of Ferdinand Porsche. As early as 1941, Krupp was commissioned to design a particularly heavy tank, but none of the proposed models, which ranged between 72 and 170 tonnes, were actually realised. The initially planned code name for the project, 'Mammoth,' was changed to 'Maus' for reasons of secrecy.

The invasion of the Soviet Union in 1941 revealed to the Wehrmacht the true situation regarding the power of Soviet tanks. Hitler and his staff came to the obvious consideration that by the spring of 1943 the Red Army would be equipped with even heavier armoured vehicles. Thus, on 5 March 1942, during a conversation with Albert Speer, the Reich Minister of Armaments, Hitler stipulated that Krupp should design a tank of at least 100 tonnes, and no longer just a 72-tonne tank. The Maus would eventually go as high as 200 tonnes.

▲ The German super tank Maus; this one pictured is the only model left that was captured by the Russians.

Panzer VII Maus experimental tank - camo version.

The final weight of the 'Maus', initially planned at 150 tonnes, in fact increased to 188 tonnes for the V1 prototype and 187 tonnes for the V2, due to the continuous increase in armour to 220 mm. This created significant difficulties for the motorisation. Despite its already impressive size, the 'Maus' was later surpassed in weight by the P-1000 and P-1500 'Monster' projects.

On 21 March of the same year, Hitler extended the assignment to Porsche, which was given an independent contract to develop a model of the same weight.

In 1942, the project accelerated and the first components, such as hulls and turrets, began to be produced at Krupp. At a conference in January 1943, the two competing designs were presented and Hitler expressed his preference for the Porsche design. It was decided to arm the vehicle with the 12.8 cm KwK cannon, to produce 10 units per month and to assign final assembly to Altmärkische Kettenwerke (Alkett). The Mäus and Tiger II were the weapons destined to ensure the Wehrmacht's technological superiority for 1944.

However, an air attack on 4 August 1943 seriously damaged the Krupp factory, causing delays, while the technical solutions for the engine, chassis and armament were not yet ready. At the time, the production line was already based on a few dozen units. This made it clear that more time would be needed before the project could be completed, and it was not until 1944 that the first driving tests could be carried out. Not only did these wartime mishaps lead to a substantial overall redesign of the project, so it is easy to speak of the Maus II project from here on in. In a way this was fortunate, as this setback allowed light to be shed on some serious errors, such as the oversized hulls, which were too wide for the Reich's rails! Towards the end of 1944, the only two prototypes made (five other frames lay incomplete) were transferred to the military research centre in Kummersdorf, where the Wehrmacht carried out tests. But in reality, that summer bombing ended the adventure and by the end of 1943, the idea of the Maus had died before it was born. With the Russians at the gates, the prototypes were destroyed. The remains of the vehicles were later recovered by the Red Army, which sent them to Kubinka for further inspection and testing.

DATA SHEET - PANZER VIII MAUS (topo)	
Type	Heavy tank
Lenght	1009 cm
Width	367 cm
Height	371 cm
Setting date	1945
Weight in combat order	188 t
Crew	6 (commander, driver, 1 radio operator, 2 servants and gunner)
Engine	Daimler-Benz MB 509 794 kW (1080 CV)
Maximum speed	20 km/h on road 10 km/h off road
Autonomy	160 km
Producer	Ferdinand Porsche
Armouring	From 60 to 280 mm
Armament	1 128 mm KwK 44 L/55 gun, 1 75 mm L36/5 gun 1-2 MG 34 7.92 mm machine guns
Production	2

Panzer VII Maus experimental tank - camo version.

TECHNICAL SPECIFICATIONS

Engine and traction The Maus used a hybrid petrol-electric or diesel-electric traction system. A combustion engine powered an electric generator that transmitted energy to two motors for movement. This configuration was necessary to handle the vehicle's massive weight, which exceeded 180 tonnes in the final prototypes.

The main armament of the Maus consisted of a 12.8 cm KwK cannon, with an elevation range of -7° to +23°, of the type already used on the Jagdtiger. It was also flanked by a 7.5 cm secondary cannon for light targets and an MG42 machine gun for infantry on the left side. The turret, equipped with armour up to 220 mm thick, made the Maus virtually immune to most enemy shells of the time. A large number of smoke candles completed the equipment. The vehicle was also equipped with a futuristic fire suppression system, which was extremely rare on armoured vehicles of the Second World War. However, this additional protection system gradually increased the weight of the Maus, further limiting its mobility.

TESTING AND FINAL DESTINY

Testing by Porsche began in November 1943 at the Kummersdorf test centre, with diving and towing tests. and shooting tests at the Army Research Institute in Hillersleben, but were always hampered by constant mechanical problems and Allied bombing. The two completed prototypes were then taken to Böblingen for further evaluation.

Without engine and turret, chassis 205/2, arrived in Böblingen on 10 March 1944. On the following 3 May 1944, the turret arrived, but still without the two guns. After the guns were installed, they were assembled for the first time on 9 June 1944 by mechanics from the Krupp company. The photos show that the only existing turret was then mounted on the 2nd chassis and the entire vehicle was given a three-colour camouflage paint job. Ready for a final test, the two prototypes were brought back to Kummersdorf. At the end of the conflict, both vehicles were destroyed by German forces to prevent their capture. However, the remains were recovered by the Red Army, which transported them to Kubinka, where one of the vehicles was reconstructed by combining the hull of the first prototype with the turret of the second. After Soviet tests on the vehicle after its capture, the Maus was exhibited at the Tank Museum in Kubinka, where it is still preserved today as a testimony to German war technology.

▲ The German super tank Maus, being camouflaged by Wermacht gunners.

March 1946 Intelligence Bulletin, Col[n]

Panzer VII Maus experimental tank - underwater version. Above: sketch of the original design.

MILITARY CONSIDERATIONS

Although the Maus was a technological masterpiece, it had serious operational limitations:
The main disadvantages were the maximum speed of 13 km/h off-road and a total weight of almost 190 tonnes, which made it virtually impossible to pass over bridges. The vehicle was therefore more of a mobile bunker than a tank useful in mobile and fast warfare. In the event of a retreat, there would have been no possibility of a quick evacuation; the rat would have had to be left behind, abandoned and blown up. In the event of an attack, it would not have been able to keep up with the rapid advance. Although the Maus would have been a big problem for the enemy because of its firepower and armour, it could have been outflanked, surrounded and captured, which is why the use of accompanying tanks was considered. The enormous need for fuel posed another problem, especially since by the end of the war the Germans were severely short of fuel. Furthermore, this mobile fortress could only be transported on a special 14-axle railway carriage and even then could not pass through tunnels or railway bridges. In short, although impressive in power and protection, its inefficiency decreed its complete uselessness on the battlefield.

▲ Two pictures of the Maus, during testing and in rail transport with the special pallet.

▲ The German super tank Maus just captured by the Russians and tested by them.

◄ Left: view of the vehicle as it was found; the German engineers blew it up so as not to leave this weapon, which had cost so many sacrifices, in enemy hands.

▲ British photo after the surrender in 1945, showing an unfinished Maus turret in a tank factory.

▲ Various views of the Maus and details of the model in the Russian museum in Kubinka. Wiki cc1.

CONCLUSIONS

When it comes to military land vehicles, no machine embodies power and terror like a tank. The pinnacle of armoured engineering, tanks were born during the First World War as rudimentary steel behemoths on tracks, armed with cannons and intended to shatter enemy lines. But from those humble beginnings, they evolved rapidly, and just over 20 years later during World War II, tanks became the vanguards of destruction, leading infantry into battles, probing enemy movements and engaging in fierce duels with their counterparts.

It was in that titanic conflict that German tanks, such as the legendary Tiger I, rose to become a symbol of invincibility. The concept of a heavy tank already existed, but it was the Tiger that embodied the pinnacle of lethality: an armoured monster, almost impregnable thanks to its fortress-thick armour, capable of annihilating any opponent with a devastating blow.

Nobody did better than German engineering in this field in those years. The Germans researched and produced countless armoured vehicles and technologically advanced weapons. In addition to the Panzer IV, V, the Tiger I and II, the formidable tank fighters, heavy self-propelled artillery such as the Ferdinand. German technology produced megalomaniac designs, often involving war propaganda to which these feats were no strangers. Thus were born many examples of experimental tanks discussed here.

Of all of them, there was a German tank that pushed this concept to its extreme limits, so daring and colossal that it remains unmatched to this day. That tank was the Maus. Although it never entered production, its existence represents an extraordinary feat of engineering, a monument to wartime megalomania. The Panzer VIII Maus, the heaviest tank ever built, is still surrounded by an aura of legend today, and its secrets continue to amaze.

▲ The terrible destruction caused by the Allied bombing of the Krupp factories.

CAMOUFLAGE AND DISTINCTIVE SIGNS

In the early stages of the war in Poland and France, the German army mainly used vehicles painted in Dunkelgrau (RAL 7021), with some vehicles also painted in Dunkelbraun (RAL 7017) as a camouflage motif until the Oberkommando des Heeres decided that only Dunkelgrau should be used. The decision did not only apply to tanks, but also to all other vehicles or AFVs: armoured cars, half-tracks and even kitchen tanks were painted the same colour.

This Dunkelgrau is often shown in illustrations not too correctly. The point is that it is in reality a very dark bluish-grey colour. This erroneous fact is often due to the fact that grey tends to "blend" effectively with the surrounding colours and consequently appear much lighter.

The war fought, however, opened the eyes of Hitler's generals, especially in Russia and Africa. In both theatres of operation, Dunkelgrau could be seen miles away, a clear invitation to enemy fire. Therefore, the German divisions in the USSR used any useful material to colour their vehicles white, including natural materials such as chalk, sheets, piled snow and the inevitable whitewash. The resulting camouflage saved the skin of many a tank driver....

These amateurish bleaches also had the advantage that they gradually washed away with the late winter and early spring rains, melting like snow. The same problem in Libya, although here white was not needed, a solution was worked out with typical German stubbornness and finally a solution was found when Gelbbraun (RAL 8000) was assigned to that front and the vehicles in Dunkelgrau were quickly camouflaged with the desert. In addition to colouring in Gelbraun, Graugrün (RAL 7008) was also used in Africa, the latter in different variants conditioned by what the tank drivers had on hand, or what they managed to capture from the enemy.

Starting in 1942, official colours began to be in short supply at the front and often also at the factory. Military vehicles were therefore painted using copies or alternative colour schemes, especially for desert vehicles (more isolated than the homeland), using Braun (RAL 8020) and Grau (brown and grey, RAL 7027). On the pages of the book you will find a very clear mirror on these colours and the RAL designation.

In addition to Africa, vehicles painted in the two-tone camouflage already in use in the desert also began to be used on the Eastern Front. It must be remembered, however, that in mid-war most German tanks in Russia were still Dunkelgrau, at least until 1943, when the OKH issued a new order that the standard basic colour of all vehicles became Dunkelgelb (dark yellow, RAL 7028). The colour was not a true yellow, but rather tended towards bronze. A delicate colour, however, that varied, even enormously, depending on many factors: who painted it, how much it was diluted with solvents, time, wear and tear, etc. RAL 7028 offers, even in the bibliography, a large number of 'variants'!

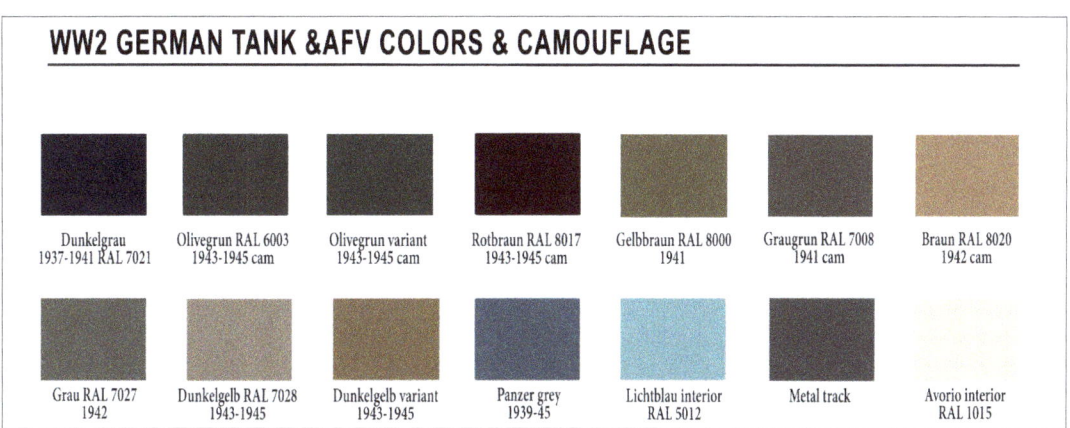

So it was partly by chance, partly by luck that they came up with the modern camouflage that the Germans called the *Hinterhalt-Tarnung* or '*Ambush*'. A complicated aspect to describe, but in fact it is an effect of light filtered through natural foliage, in short, a very effective camouflage. As with works of art, one could also speak of styles, as varied as possible. One was reminiscent of the *pointillisme* of the French Impressionists. A more 'orphic' one also called disc or mottled. The choice of one style or the other was also to a certain extent the signature of the factory that produced the vehicles (from mid-1944 the vehicles were painted in the production plants). The colours applied in the factory were a base of Dunkelgelb, with patches of Rotbraun (red brown) and Olivgrün (olive green). Storage problems, thunderstorms and other problems arose that made the outgoing supply varied.

Finally, in December 1944, a new order was issued that the tanks were to be painted all over with a base coat (over the red-oxide primer, the Italian minio) of Dunkelgrün and/or Olivgrün with applications of Dunkelgelb and Rotbraun stripes and stains, and this seems to be the last order given for camouflage while the war was in progress.

The application of camouflage was generally done with compressed-air paint sprays, failing which it was done 'the old-fashioned way': brushes, mops or simply rags on the end of a stick. These artifices, this art of contrivance ended up multiplying the camouflage variants that would later be destined for the battlefield. Like all armies, the German army had realised (often before many) that concealing vehicles in defensive or offensive manoeuvres would increase the likelihood of surviving the clash. In addition to the camouflage painted on the vehicle itself, foliage (branches, bushes, hay, even stacks of wood) was therefore often used to cover the vehicle, usually from the front, to make it even more difficult to detect and distinguish from its surroundings. More rarely, tarpaulins and camouflage nets mixed with foliage were also used to further conceal the tank. Last but not least, mud and snow were also a cheap, but effective, camouflage that was very useful for blending in with the surroundings.

▲ A tank driver intent on colouring the camouflage of his vehicle (an Sd.Kfz 173) with spray. Bundesarchiv.

▲ The experimental VK 4502 Hinten tank, made by Walter Ferrari of the Pumenengo (BG) modelling club.

BIBLIOGRAPHY

- Mr A I Bruce. *"Gw Tiger für 17 cm K 72 (Sf)"*. Wehrmacht-history.com. Archived from the original on 2017-10-07. Retrieved 2012-07-01.
- P. Chamberlain and H. Doyle (1978) *Encyclopedia of German Tanks of World War Two – Revised Edition*, Arms and Armor press.
- D. Doyle (2005). *German military Vehicles*, Krause Publications.
- D. Nešić, (2008), *Naoružanje Drugog Svetsko Rata*-Nemačka, Beograd
- T. Anderson (2018) *History of the Panzejager, Volume 1 Origin and evolution 1939-42*, Osprey Publishing.
- T.L. Jentz and H.L. Doyle (1997) *Panzer Tracts No.4 Panzerkampfwagen IV*
- T.L. Jentz and H.L. Doyle (2004) *Panzer Tracts No.7-1 Panzerjager*
- *"Panzerkampfwagen VII Löwe (Lion)"*. Achtung Panzer. 1996.
- B. David *"Panzerkampfwagen VII Löwe (VK 70.01) Heavy tank – Paper project (1942)"*. Retrieved 23 July 2017.
- Jentz, Tom; Doyle, Hilary (2001). *Panzer Tracts No.20-1: Paper Panzers – Panzerkampfwagen, Sturmgeschuetz and Jagdpanzer.*
- George Forty, *Tiger Tank Battalions in World War II*, Zenith Imprint, 2009.
- F. M. von Senger und Etterlin: *Die deutschen Panzer 1926–1945*. Bernard & Graefe Verlag, 1998
- Walter J. Spielberger, Hilary L.Doyle: *Der Panzer-Kampfwagen Tiger und seine Abarten*. In: *Militärfahrzeuge*. 6. Auflage. Band 7. Motorbuch Verlag, Stuttgart 1998,
- Thomas L. Jentz & Hilary Louis Doyle: *Panzerkampfwagen VI P (Sd.Kfz. 181) - Porsche Typ 100 and 101*. 1. Auflage. Darlington Productions Inc., Darlington 1997.
- Fritz Hahn: *Waffen und Geheimwaffen des deutschen Heeres 1933–1945*. Dörfler-Verlag,
- Walter J. Spielberger: *Spezial-Panzer-Fahrzeuge des deutschen Heeres. Militärfahrzeuge Band 8*. Motorbuch-Verlag, Stuttgart 1977,
- Ferdinand M. von Senger und Etterlin, Franz Kosar, Walter J. Spielberger: *Die deutschen Panzer 1926–1945*. Bernard & Graefe, Bonn 1998
- Michael Sawodny, Kai Bracher: *Panzerkampfwagen Maus und andere deutsche Panzerprojekte*. Podzun-Pallas, Wölfersheim-Berstadt 1998
- Lothar Boschen, Jürgen Barth: *Das große Buch der Porsche-Sondertypen und -Konstruktionen von 1931 bis heute*. 1. Auflage. Motorbuch Verlag, Stuttgart 1984
- Thomas L. Jentz, Hilary Louis Doyle: *Schwerer Panzerkampfwagen Maus and E 100 – Panzer Tracts No. 6-3*. Panzer Tracts, Boyds, MD 2008, ISBN 0-9815382-3-1
- Karl R. Pawlas: *Panzerkampfwagen Maus* - Journal Verlag Schwend, Schwäbisch Hall 1975
- *Panzerkampfwagen VI Tiger (P) VK4501(P)/Porsche Typ 101*, su achtungpanzer.com
- *VK4501(P) Panzer VI*, su wehrmacht-history.com.
- *SdKfz 181 Panzerkampfwagen VI Tiger I (PzKpfW VI/Pz 6) Heavy Tank*, su militaryfactory.com.
- *Pz Kpfw Tiger (P)*, su panzerworld.com.
- *Baubericht - Panzerkampfwagen VI(P) "Porsche-Tiger", VK 4501(P)*, su panzer-modell.de.

ALREADY PUBLISHED TITLES

ALL BOOKS IN THE SERIES ARE PRINTED IN ITALIAN AND ENGLISH

VISIT OUR WEBSITE FOR MORE INFORMATION ON
THE WEAPONS ENCYCLOPAEDIA:
https://soldiershop.com/collane/libri/the-weapons-encyclopaedia/

TWE-032 EN

www.ingramcontent.com/pod-product-compliance
Lightning Source LLC
LaVergne TN
LVHW072121060526
838201LV00068B/4939